For Holly

This Christmas is going to be better than best!

It will definitely out-sparkle the rest!

Why you ask?

Please let me explain...

Because I can't wait to see you again!

It's been a few years...

Since we've all been together!

With the entire family, in the same space.

So I think it's about time to...

JUMP JUMP JUMP
AND SAY
MERRY
CHRISTMAS
TO YOU!

Grandmas, Grandpas, Uncles, Aunts and Cousins are travelling from near and far.

Some by planes, some by trains and some by cars.

Because Christmas is a fantastic time...

To laugh and play...

To create
new memories...

Christmas is a very special once a year day!

And now it's time to...

And let's not forget the Christmas presents!

It takes hard work to get them all here!

Thanks to Santa and his elves we've never missed a year!

And let's not forget Santa's reindeer!

There will be lots of yummy food to eat!

And Christmas Pudding will be so sweet!

Giving and receiving gifts is so much fun!

And of course there will be something for everyone!

So now it's time to...

JUMP JUMP JUMP

AND SAY

MERRY

CHRISTMAS

TO YOU!

MERRY CHRISTMAS!

FROM ALL OF US TO ALL OF YOU!

Jump Series:
Jump Like a Caribou!
Jump Like a Kangaroo!
Jump at the Zoo!
Jump and Say P.U.!
Jump and Say Boo!
Jump and Say Valentine's Day Is
For Kids Too!
Jump and Look For a Clue!
Jump and Say Happy Birthday to You!
Jump For Everything Blue!
Jump, Hop and Say Happy Easter To
You!
Jump and Say Cock-A-Doodle-Do!
Jump and Sing Da-Do-Do-Do!
Jump and Ask Who? Who?
Jump and Squawk Like a Cockatoo!
Jump and Ask Is It You or Ewe?
Jump and Say There's an Ewww in My
Stew!
Jump and Cheer Happy New Year!
Jump and Say There's a Moo-Moo in a
Tutu!
Jump and Say There's a Hare in My
Hair!

Jump and Say My Aunt Ate An Ant!
Jump and Say There's An Aardvark In The
Amusement Park!
Jump and Buzz Like A Bee!

Clap For Series
Clap for 1!
Clap for 2!
Clap for 3!
Clap for 4!
Clap for 5!
Clap for 6!
Clap for 7!
Clap for 8!
Clap for 9!
Clap for 10!

The Cat Who Said Hello
The Three Boulders
Billy Shakespeare
Billie Shakespeare
Learn To Draw With Symmetry
ABC More Learn to Draw With Symmetry

Non-Fiction
103 Fundraising Ideas For Parent Volunteers With
Schools and Teams